APPROACHING
ABBA

APPROACHING ABBA

A 31 DAY DEVOTIONAL

Robin Conrad Sturm

Illustrated by Nicki Scolaro Bland

For Fiona, for feeding the lambs.

CONTENTS

Introduction 1

Signed and Sealed 4

Grab the Ball 8

Tell Me a Story 12

Get Close 16

Come as a Child 20

The Truth's Roar 24

Follow the Scent 28

Did You Call Me? 32

Are You Still My Friend? 36

Laughing All the Way 40

Strong and Tall 44

Sew and So 48

It's Okay, I Trust You! 52

Smile for the Camera 56

Falling Into the Foam 60

But I Don't Want to Freeze! 64

Hey, You Promised! 68

Baby Videos 72

Are You Afraid of the Dark? 76

Holding Dreams in Your Fist 80

Deeper and Higher 84

Peek-a Boo! I See You! 88

Parting Gifts 92

Where's the Caboose? 96

God's Treasures 100

Could You Repeat That? .104

Getting Over the Hurdle .108

Dancing Squirrels 112

Is Perfection Perfect? 116

Reaching Up 120

Monsters in My Room 124

Author Biography 129

INTRODUCTION

> *"Then Jesus called for the children and said to the disciples,*
> *"Let the children come to me. Don't stop them!*
> *For the Kingdom of God belongs to those*
> *who are like these children."*

—Luke 18:16

What is it about small children that the Son of God Himself, our Savior, singled them out as examples of how to approach Him – to approach God?

The name Abba doesn't just mean the closest of relationships to our Father; it does not mean "Daddy." The Hebrew word is derived from its parallel origin in Aramaic, and it means two things: intimacy and obedience. Abba is the closest term of endearment for the person who knows us inside and out, even before we were born, and loves us with such depth that it's beyond our scope of understanding. It is only used by the intimately close child whose obedience is willing and absolute to the absolute Authority.

The concept of the word Abba is an entire Bible study in itself, but, for the purpose of this devotional, we will focus on

the fact that Jesus wants us to see why He told us to be like little children to approach our Father.

After spending some years working in a preschool, I can see that the many complex layers of these tiny people are the keys to a closer, deeper understanding of an indescribable relationship with God, our true Father. He knows us so intimately, yet our understanding of Him is fleeting and superficial by comparison.

My hope in writing this devotional is that it will inspire you to start a journey – a journey to deepen your desire for the absolute closest relationship and the secure freedom of total obedience with God our Father, the Son, and the Holy Spirit – intimate enough to truly call Him Abba.

THOUGHTS

SIGNED AND SEALED

I teach in a preschool. For many people, that conjures up sounds of constant chatter, many tears, and hours of play amidst carpets, walls, and toys, all in bright, primary colors. Pretty basic, right? Nothing could be further from the truth. There are indeed bright colors, and yes, the chatter can get out of hand if the teachers don't have a strong routine and curriculum to follow. However, the learning is far from basic. It may not be complex, but especially for the teachers, the lessons become very profound.

At the end of one particular day, I arrived home and saw that my ankles had been decorated with lines of green Sharpie. I had been completely unaware that a little four-year-old girl in my class had decided to "tag" me. I had been reading a story to several children. Two were sharing my lap, and one was standing by my left shoulder. I was not focused on my ankles. When I finished the story, the tiny artist down at my feet proudly announced, "I wrote my name on your ankles, so now you're mine!" Aside from wishing I had worn socks that day, I felt kind of warm knowing that a little girl had signed her name on my ankles and called dibs on me.

We are not meant to navigate life totally alone and isolated. However, that doesn't mean we can't be independent or

live on our own, but there is a natural sense of belonging and identification that God put within each of us that makes us long for fellowship. That fellowship and connection with other people is wonderful, but that longing was originally meant to be a desire for fellowship with God, our Father, our Abba.

When the little girl tagged me, she was setting me apart as hers. She was telling me she loved me and wanted to claim me as her own, even though I was unaware that she was doing it.

God chooses us as His own long before we are even aware of who He is. He created us and tagged us to be His children, and He lovingly wants fellowship with us. We are often not aware of Him, but He is always here and ready to spend as much time with us as we want. So, take some time, crawl into His lap, and let Him tell You how much He loves you.

Father God, thank You for claiming me as Your child before I was even born. Thank You for wanting to spend time with me every day. Please help me to remember that You are constantly by my side, every moment, and our relationship together means that I am never totally alone.

In Jesus' name. Amen.

THOUGHTS

GRAB THE BALL

Learning to catch a big rubber ball is a developmental marker for small children. When they first attempt a game of catch, they basically just stare at the ball as it's gently tossed to them, allow it to bounce off their chest, and then run to pick it up as it rolls away. A bit further along the way, they do try to catch the ball, but they snap their arms shut too late as the ball again just bounces off their chest and rolls away. Maybe their heart isn't really in the game.

More time passes, and I was playing catch with a small circle of four-year-old children. A couple of them had gotten really good – others not so much. For the little ones who were still struggling, the real issue seemed to be fear. They would eagerly hold their hands out as the ball flew towards them, but just as they were about to make contact, they would squeeze their eyes shut, turn their heads away, and slap the ball down.

So, here's what we did: I told them, "The next time the ball gets close, instead of turning away and waiting for it to hit you in the face, you already know it's coming, so reach out and grab that ball right out of the air!"

It worked! These proud little achievers learned how to take the initiative and snatch that ball that they knew was coming right to them. They grabbed it in mid-air!

How many times have you prayed and asked God for something, and then doubt and fear took over, you turned your face, and then slapped God's answer away?

When God is tossing us a blessing or an answer to prayer, or a mission, or a Word just for us, often we let fear tell us that it's too hard, or we didn't hear Him correctly, or it's too good to be true, so we must be mistaken. God wants us to grab His gifts with confidence and to hold on tight. His aim is perfect, and every gift from God is good, so be careful to not slap His gift away. Our Father is a loving, giving God, who is teaching us to grab and trust all that He gives to us.

Father, I truly *am* Your child. Even saying it out loud seems
impossible. Please help me to receive all of Your blessings with
true gratefulness. Please keep me from rejecting or slapping away
anything from You, for You have every detail of my life planned
from the beginning. You want only the best for me because I AM
YOUR CHILD.

In Jesus' name. Amen.

TELL ME A STORY

It's no secret that small children have a difficult time sitting still for long periods of time. A child's forté is perpetual motion – and discovery. One of the biggest challenges in a preschool is to teach skills in a way that feels like a game. Just when you think you have found a game that is teaching the letter, or the number, or the skill of the day, the children quickly get bored and are ready to move on to the next activity. A preschool teacher needs a lot of tricks up her sleeve to keep the kids on the right course and encourage their desire to learn.

HOWEVER … sit on the floor and start quietly reading a book with colorful pictures to one small child, and without any effort another child comes over to listen, then another plops into your lap, then another sits close with his head on your shoulder, and you have reeled them in. Before you know it, fifteen children are quieter than they have been all day and are listening intently to the words in the book. They may have the book at home and may have heard it many times, but they still want to be close and hear it again. They remember every word; they can say it with you, and they still want to sit and listen. And the longer they sit and listen, the closer they press in.

God has a wonderful story to tell us. It's exciting; it's comforting; it tells us about where we came from. It tells us about

incredible miracles; it shows us how we are loved beyond measure, and it reveals the assurance of how to live forever in Paradise. Best of all, it's one hundred percent true!

Spend some time on our Father's lap and listen to Him tell you a story. You have heard the words before, but the promises they hold are faithfully true every time you hear them. Read along with Him; He loves for you to be able to say the words with Him. God loves you? to repeat them. They often sound brand new in different ways, and the more you sit and listen to Him, the closer you can become to your heavenly Father as you press in.

*"Call to Me and I will answer you and tell you great
and unsearchable things you do not know."*

—Jeremiah 33:3

*"Anyone who belongs to God listens gladly to the words of
God. But you don't listen because you don't belong to God."*

—John 8:47

O Father, I want to hear You tell me a story. I want to gladly sit
with You and hear You tell me all the things I don't know or have
forgotten. I belong to You; I am Your child, and I want to get
closer to You and hear Your voice.

In Jesus' name. Amen.

THOUGHTS

GET CLOSE

I believe that if everyone was required to teach one year of preschool when they reach twenty-one years old, they would learn the secrets of having a close relationship with God and each other from the best teachers in the world: the children. In their blessed naiveté, children don't know how wise they are, yet they are infinitely profound.

- Everything is manageable if your best friend is doing it, too.
- Having rules and boundaries keeps us safe.
- We need to stop and help someone who has fallen down and is crying before moving on with our friends.
- It really *is* more fun sometimes to just play the game and laugh, rather than keep score to see who won.
- It's very important to finish our work before going out to play … most of the time.
- The most important piece of wisdom is: It's nice knowing you can sit next to someone you like, even when you don't talk.

One day, my preschool class was sitting in a circle getting ready to hear a story. As an assistant to the teacher, I was sitting

in different places to work with children who needed help, support, or encouragement. There was one little boy who was extremely lively and loud on the playground, but during class time he consistently, quietly, and conscientiously would get his work done. I'm sure he had his emotional moments at home; he was a four-year-old, but in school he was a model student. On this particular day, I sat down by him, and he leaned over to whisper to me, "I like it when you sit next to me." He quickly pulled up his pant leg to reveal his new dinosaur socks, and then he turned his complete attention to the story. He didn't say another word the entire time; he just needed reassurance that he wasn't alone, and I knew I had a new little friend.

We were not created to be comfortable existing alone, separated from others. It doesn't mean we can't be comfortable *living* alone, but our lives were not meant to be lived in isolation. In order to relate to each other, we must lean in and instigate contact. God says that all we need to do to get closer to Him is to take a step in his direction. For some reason, with each other, we often build walls: We set expectations; we make comparisons; we set rules; we practically audition people before we allow them to enter our bubble. All of those self-imposed conditions will hardly foster trust in each other because we will always fail at something and eventually disappoint each other. It's wonderful to know that God expects nothing from us except our desire to get close to Him.

The little boy in the preschool class said it best when he simply whispered, "I like it when you sit next to me."

God loves it; He's waiting patiently, and He whispers to us every day, "I like it when you sit next to me, even if you don't talk."

"Draw near to God, and He will draw near to you."

—James 4:8

Lord, thank You for always being ready to hold me close to You, whether I want to talk or just rest my head on Your shoulder. Thank You for *always* being near to me and wanting me to get closer.

In Jesus' name. Amen.

THOUGHTS

COME AS A CHILD

When the day is over at the preschool where I teach, I love to watch the little faces of the children as they file out the door to the pick-up area. They are eagerly and hopefully searching the crowd for the familiar face that they know loves them so well, whether it's Mom or Dad, maybe Grandma or Grandpa, sometimes a much-admired sister. The children carefully walk down the slate steps with their heavy backpacks bouncing up and down, some of them beginning to look a bit apprehensive if they don't immediately see the someone who is there just for them.

But then, one by one, like stars appearing in the twilight sky, little faces light up; they dump their heavy backpacks on the sidewalk behind them, and they go racing out and leaping out to the waiting hands that pluck them out of the air and hold them close. They eventually retrieve their backpacks and start to empty out their cares of the day: their artwork, their triumphs, their boo-boos, their tears, their giggles – all of it comes rushing out of their hearts as they work their way home, because they are so aware that the people who love them think they are important and significant.

God uses little ones such as these as examples of how He wants us to come to Him – without fear, with perfect trust, and

dropping our burdens from our backs to leap into His arms. He wants *our* faces to eagerly and expectantly be searching for Him. He wants us to tell Him everything: what we're excited about, our desires, our hopes, what is scaring us, what we are furious about, what disappointed us today. He already knows, but He wants to hear our heart, because He is our most trusted confidante, and He wants us to let *Him* carry that heavy burden we've been lugging. He also knows we may get so very angry at Him from time to time. I see the kids sometimes wail in protest at their parents when things aren't going the way they expect or want. But Mom and Dad love them desperately, no matter what tantrum must be endured on the car ride home and what words are spewed at them, because their job is to do what their children really need at the moment.

God wants us to be as excited to see him every day as the children are to see their parents – to come to Him with every care, every story, every fear, everything that is in our heart; it doesn't matter to Him if we're throwing a tantrum in protest over what's happening. He wants us to tell Him because He wants us to trust Him, and we are *very* significant to Him. He's not far away, even when we're apprehensive that we're not seeing Him immediately. However, he is always ready and waiting as we race to tell Him about our day. He knows we may throw a tantrum now and then, and He also knows what words escape from our lips in that anger … He really does know, and He will *always* respond to us with love.

His arms are open – He's waiting.

—Matthew 19:14

Abba Father, please help me learn to see You first, to talk to You first, to run to You first with everything that's on my heart. I want to drop all my burdens and cares right now, knowing You will help me to sort through them one by one. I want to look forward to running straight to You every day, because I know You love me, and I want to share my heart as Your loving child.

In Jesus' name. Amen.

THOUGHTS

THE TRUTH'S ROAR

One of the things I find so intriguing about young children is their unabashed ability to say and do whatever is on their minds with absolutely no forethought nor restraint. When they're being reprimanded for inappropriate behavior, they don't seem to be embarrassed; they just seem to wonder why everyone else is so upset.

I learned a profound lesson from one of my preschool classes while on the playground. One little boy discovered just how much fun it was to run up to a smaller girl (smaller than he was) and roar as loudly as he could right in her face. It would scare her to pieces; she would cry pitifully, and eventually she started running for cover as soon as the little boy looked like he was just thinking about approaching her. The "roar-er" was persisting and not responding in the least to our usual teacher inter ventions, and the "cry-er" was more afraid than ever. So I told her that the next time the roar-er unleashed his self-proclaimed power on her, she should just put her little hands on her hips, take a deep breath, and roar at him with every bit of strength her tiny body could muster.

So we waited. It didn't take long. The roar-er saw her standing alone, and he decided to make his move toward her. He opened his mouth and began to unleash a sound that could send

God's angels racing up to heaven. The other teacher and I called out to the cry-er, "Do it! Do it now!" And she did. Her adversary increased his decibels, and she momentarily flinched. However, she decided she was done being scared. Our little hero stuck out her tiny chin and screamed, and screamed, and screamed some more, right back at the roar-er with her newly discovered strength. Then it happened. The little roar-er had been completely caught off-guard; he looked very disappointed, and then he ran off to play another game. Our little cry-er became our little victor, and she looked as surprised as the roar-er … but not nearly as disappointed. As a matter of fact, she looked quite pleased with herself.

Do you have monsters and roaring dragons in your life that cause you to turn and run as their shadows approach, even before they reach your doorstep? I think we all do. Their roars and threats conjure up our own perceptions of undefeatable monsters. However, their only real strength is the sound of their voice. Their power is no match for the real power and confidence that God has made available to us. Our experiences make us stronger. The support of our friends and family is stronger. Strongest of all is our Advocate, Jesus Christ, and His truths. Sometimes our monsters and dragons may wear down and retreat, and sometimes they may continue to roar for what my seem like forever. But they will never win and destroy us or who we are as long as our integrity, character, and faith remain intact. As long as we know Who is really fighting our battles, those dragon's roars are just loud noise.

So next time a monster begins to roar in your life, look it squarely in the face, put your hands defiantly on your hips, and roar with all your might. Those monsters are just looming shadows that get shorter as God's light in your life gets brighter. God's truth in you is the real strength that speaks in the silence and will cut through the loudest fear.

*"Do not fear, for I am with you.
Do not anxiously look about you, for I am your God.
I will strengthen you; surely I will help you;
surely I will uphold you with my righteous right hand."*

—Isaiah 41:10

My Lord, I put my trust in You alone. I want to let You take the lead and fight my battles, because I know You are my true source of strength."

In Jesus' name. Amen.

THOUGHTS

FOLLOW THE SCENT

At the end of one of the days at preschool, the mom of a student in my class told me that she knew her little boy was loved and felt secure at school because he smelled of my perfume when he came home every day. She had evidence of where he had been and whom he had been close to. So, I started to wonder what lingers on *us* that reveals where we have been. What influences from other people have become a part of who we are? What have we left with other people? There are some things, like our attitude or demeanor, that we absorb and transfer to others without ever realizing it.

So, who are you reflecting or picking up in your everyday life? Are you spending enough time with your Heavenly Father to pick up His family traits? Whose attitudes, habits, or personality are you resembling and passing on to others? Family members don't just look like each other. Mannerisms and habits often reveal family connections; accents in speech give away where someone grew up. There are so many things that can disclose how people are linked to each other.

There are also clues that reveal someone's priorities. Attributes and qualities show where someone derives his or her

strength and who has contributed to forming that person's character. We can try faking what we think others want to hear or see, but that won't last – the truth eventually comes out, often at the most inconvenient or embarrassing times!

Parents of teens have always been concerned about who their kids are with, and which friends are good or bad influences. Kids, as well as adults, like to be known by their circle of friends; they want to be with the cool crowd.

God is the cool crowd. The Father, the Son, and the Holy Spirit are the crowd that will leave a lingering fragrance on you that will change and redeem lives.

Are you the one that people want to emulate, that leaves a telltale trail or clue as to Whom you spend your time with? When you speak, does your accent give away Who your family is, or what Kingdom is your real home? When people look at you, do they see how much you look like your Father – your Abba? Lots of questions, but only one answer.

*"So all of us who have had the veil removed can see
and reflect the glory of the Lord. And the Lord –
who is the Spirit – makes us more and more like
Him as we are changed into His glorious image."*

—2 Corinthians 3:18

Father God, help me to reflect You; help me to leave Your fragrance behind me. I want to spend so much time with You that I pick up the "family resemblance." I want to have your accent when I speak; I want people to know I am a citizen of Your Kingdom. I want other people to want to be a part of our family.

In Jesus' name. Amen.

THOUGHTS

DID YOU CALL ME?

All of us have a desire to know we're significant and to know we have a true purpose. We want to be noticed by someone … by anyone.

A little boy in the preschool class did not like playing alone – ever. He avoided it whenever he could. He often needed to be encouraged to concentrate on his classwork alone, rather than trying to make it a group effort.

A different little guy was very happy doing puzzles and playing alone during free time; he went so far as to try to do the group projects alone. He needed to be reminded to work with his group and contribute his imagination to the team. He wasn't lonely at all, just very content on his own. He sometimes would get so deeply engrossed in his quiet alone time that he wouldn't hear his name being called the first several times. The first, very gregarious little boy would get so involved creating an imaginary yet very noisy crowd that his name needed to be called many times before he was aware of another voice in the room. Neither child was deliberately ignoring the teacher; they were both submerged in the happy world they had created for themselves.

We do that, too. We sometimes feel the need to create our own world where we feel significant and needed. In this stressful world, that brings us comfort.

We often fail to hear our name being called when God is trying to tell us something, but we're completely self-involved in our comfortable and familiar world. We all can become deaf and blind to change. God can place open doors in front of us, or be calling us to a new path, but we will turn away and retreat into the land of familiarity. We are comfortable there, and we can't hear God calling us into something different. Ah, safe.

We don't need to hear God calling loudly, just clearly. Elijah didn't hear God calling in a violent wind, or in an earthquake, or even in a huge fire. But in a gentle whisper, Elijah heard God.

If we decide to listen, whispers are the right voice we need at the right time. We whisper to our babies when they're born. We whisper precious and important secrets that we want to be kept safe. We whisper around a sleeping child. Imagine screaming in those situations!

God whispers lovingly to us, but we often forget to take the time to listen. But take the time. You will hear God calling your name – he has something to tell you.

*"The gatekeeper opens the gate for Him, and the sheep
recognize His voice and they come to Him.
He calls His own sheep by name and leads them out."*

—John 10:3

Father, thank You for creating me for special purpose. Please help me to listen and hear You calling my name. Help me to walk through the doors You open and the paths You have prepared just for me.

In Jesus' name. Amen.

THOUGHTS

ARE YOU STILL MY FRIEND?

In a preschool classroom, there are several different areas called "centers" that are designated for teaching different skills. One of those centers is for "dramatic play," where little ones learn to process social interactions with each other while engaging in make-believe everyday situations. They can be in a grocery store one day, working in a bakery on another day, putting together a birthday party, making and selling pizza, etc. Chatter is always lively and enthusiastic as the kids apply their imaginations into the scenarios and conversations that they think they hear from adults. They learn conflict resolution, forethought, organization, and all the things that would benefit adults returning to preschool for a refresher course!

One day a little girl came over to me from her art center and proudly gifted me with her latest crayon creation. I made a big fuss over her sweet generosity and skill, gave her a big hug, and she returned to her table to finish her rotation. As I turned my attention back to the dramatic play center, a real drama had begun.

I noticed that one little boy who had been working with me was sitting in a corner of the room, his tiny face turned to the wall; he was curled up like a beetle, and he was crying as though his heart was broken. I ran over to him, afraid that I had failed

to notice an injury. I knelt down next to him and asked if he had gotten hurt. He said no, still digging his face into the corner, so I asked him why he was so upset. Without turning his face to me, he sobbed, "You're not my friend anymore!" I asked, "Are you mad at me? Did I do something to upset you?" His tearful reply was, "She gave you a picture, and you hugged her, and now *she's* your friend and not me!"

Now *my* heart was breaking. This sweet little boy had yet to grasp the concept of steadfast, unconditional love. He still believed he had to earn love and acceptance. He thought he had somehow been tossed aside because someone else gave me a gift and appeared to have taken his place.

God never plays favorites. He does not base His love for us on what we bring to Him, how we act, or what rituals we have checked of our list. This devastated little boy was afraid that he had to do something or give something to be accepted and loved. He was afraid he had lost his place. When I finally was able to assure him that he was just as treasured as before, his behavior and tear-stained face immediately changed and reflected his new-found security and joy in belonging.

Once we have given our heart to Jesus Christ, we are written forever on His hand. We get to rejoice daily in our belonging to Him, because His love for us never changes, and we are safe forever with Him! We do not have to give Him anything other than our heart, and His love for us does not diminish, no matter how many others He loves. True Forever Friends!

Father, thank You for holding me safely and forever in Your comforting arms. Thank You for Your never-ending grace and love;
I am secure in knowing that nothing and no one can take me
away from You.

In Jesus' name. Amen.

THOUGHTS

LAUGHING ALL THE WAY

Winning and losing gracefully are difficult concepts for a lot of us to learn; that's why we need to start learning them early, when we're very young children.

Most little children want to stop playing when they don't win or when the winner decides to gloat – except for one little girl that I met. We were playing a board game in class, and the first time she lost, she giggled and was genuinely happy for the little boy who won. Then she turned the spinner, lost again, and giggled a bit louder. She ended up losing every time, but with each attempt she laughed louder and louder until she was actually shrieking with glee. She thought it was hilarious that she just couldn't win at this game! I had more fun watching her lose than teaching her how to play! I don't know what secret she had mastered in her four years of life so far, but that sweet little thing really knew how to love every minute of every day. Eventually, she did win a game and was certainly very happy and proud of herself, but every time her opponent won, she would yell out his victory and cheer. This little girl not only enjoyed the whole experience of working towards a goal, but she

was learning the *value* of every experience. She wasn't yet aware of her own profound wisdom, but she was already beginning to reap the benefits.

God cheers for us with every attempt and with every win. He also cheers us on for every loss because he knows how we will grow with *every* experience, and we need those tough experiences. Perhaps this little girl had faith that her time to win was coming. Your time to win is coming, too, because God has already planned it, and He has promised it. Our losses are not failures; they are the rocks that we climb up on to get a better view.

O Lord God, help me to trust You that You *do* have a plan for me that is good. Please give me stamina and persistence and hope to enjoy this journey with You, knowing that You will be rejoicing with me in everything I learn and every step I take.

In Jesus' name. Amen.

THOUGHTS

STRONG AND TALL

I have some gorgeous gladiolas grow-ing in my garden. When they bloom in early summer, the fluorescent pink blooms look stunning against the bright emerald green stems. The only problem is, as soon as the blossoms are at their biggest, they're so heavy that the entire stalk flops over to the ground. I need to tie them to a garden stake for support, so they won't be trampled or be attacked by bugs from the grass.

Like gladiolas, little children grow quickly. However, they don't grow as quickly as they'd like. They want their height to be measured often because they can't wait to get tall. Their common mantra is "I want to do it myself," but if we don't help and support them as they grow up, they won't realize their full potential; their development will be stunted, and they'll flop over and be vulnerable to the bugs and distractions of life.

God wants to support us, His dear children, to help us grow in the right direction. We tend to look to Him last, if at all, for help, or inspiration, or counsel. Tying ourselves to God like a garden stake will give us the support and guidance we need to

keep us upright, tall, and on the right path. He has designed us to shine in His gifts and reflect His beauty as we grow and bloom. Although we think it's only the children who say, "I want to do it myself," we say it to God when He is ready and waiting to stand side by side with us. When we allow ourselves to be staked to the Lord, we will be sure to grow strong, tall, and in the right direction. Our lives will reflect His beauty and point straight up to Him!

—John 15:5

Father God, I want to be closely connected to You in all I do; I want to feel Your guidance by abiding always in You. I recognize You as the source of strength in my life because I am tied to You.

In Jesus' name. Amen.

THOUGHTS

SEW AND SO

Every single gift that God gives us is for a specific purpose – His purpose. The gift is not simply to make us happy nor to build up our ego. If our gift dies when we do, then there is no far-reaching purpose; there is no legacy. The impact of our gifts is meant to be fluid and to spill over to the next generation. Our gifts are meant to affect others, to express what we feel, to teach, to influence, to bring joy, and to make people think. Most importantly, our gifts are meant to honor God.

Teaching is a gift; teaching small children is one facet of that gift. Small children absorb so quickly and remember so easily. Every act or word of encouragement from a teacher can start a child on a trajectory that might not have happened without that uplifting word at the right time. Their interest or joy in a specific activity is usually a sign of a budding gift that needs to be nurtured. The way we acknowledge and use our own gifts is one way we can teach children to honor God with theirs.

My grandmother was a professional seamstress in Russia where she was born. She immigrated to the United States when

she was a young woman, and she used her gift to make a living for herself when she arrived in America. Years later, she taught me how to sew when I was still a very little girl. Once I grew up, I needed to call upon that gift for a very special purpose.

A dear friend of mine had passed away, and her daughters gave me all the fabric that had been in her sewing closet. The gift of sewing that my grandmother passed down to me enabled me to use that fabric to make clothing for impoverished children in Colombia. Likewise, if my friend had not had the gift of sewing, she would not have had that fabric to pass on to me which I was able to turn into clothing for the children.

Many people think of sewing as an insignificant skill that no one needs anymore, because buying clothes is so much easier. It's not easier for everyone, and God uses every scrap (pun intended) of ability and talent that we are willing to turn over to Him.

Sowing seeds of inspiration and creativity into our children not only serves God, but it teaches the children how to serve, and then they teach their children, and a legacy is perpetuated.

Children are thrilled when they do a good job with their gifts. They always ask, "Do you like it? I made it for you!" We are also thrilled as adults when we do a good job. God loves it when we use His gifts. Who doesn't want to hear "Well done, good and faithful servant!" from our Father, the Creator of the Universe?

Lord, show me how to recognize the gifts You have given to me
since I was born. Show me how You want me to use them, and
please put opportunities in my path so I can use those gifts to
serve others and to honor and glorify You.

In Jesus' name. Amen.

THOUGHTS

IT'S OKAY, I TRUST YOU!

Out of their innocence, little children are so profound. One crisp winter day, when the preschool classes were over, I was waiting with one last little boy for his mother to pick him up. We were standing at the edge of the parking lot where there were still many remaining little hills of filthy snow and ice from a previous storm. This little boy was bored, so he pulled his knitted hat down over his eyes and proceeded to climb, blind, on an ice hill, yelling, "Hey, look at me!" As I ran over to pull his hat off his eyes, I called out, "You need to get down; that's not safe!" He called back to me, "No, no, it's okay! I trust you!"

Wait … What?! The other parents standing around caught the humor and laughed, and so did I, but there was something so deep in what he said. How wonderful to know that someone who loves you is always, unfailingly in control and won't let you totally fall, no matter what mistakes you make or what you want to try.

I was warmed by the fact that he trusted me, though he did kind of extend that trust all the way to presumption. I am human and can only leap so far to catch a falling child in

mid-air. However, I thought, "Do I have the capacity to have the faith of this child and to be able to trust that blindly?" One minute he'll be running to hug me with an angelic smile, and five minutes later he will need a stern lecture for balling up his fist and hitting another child. He will yell and tell me I'm not being fair, and then just a little bit later he decides to climb Mt. Freeze-a-Lot while blindfolded because he trusts how much I love him. That is confident trust.

As adults, we tell God how much we love and trust Him; then later we are shaking our fist at Him because our plans didn't work out, or there has been a door closed in our face, or we're all alone, or we feel we can't trust anyone. Maybe sometimes, our great ideas are not so great. And maybe, just maybe, we're angry at God because we don't know the end of the story He has written for us.

God knows we will make our own decisions, because the freedom to do that is one of His great gifts to us. He also knows for certain we will stumble and fall now and then, because we will always have our own slippery hills to navigate in our life. We can be assured that God loves us intensely no matter what path He leads us on, hills or not. We can say, with total confidence, "It's okay, I trust You!"

Father, please help me to put myself in the background and You in the foreground when I find myself in a difficult or lonely situation. Help me to focus on You first, to trust You always, and to remember that I don't know the end of my story that You have already written.

In Jesus' name. Amen.

THOUGHTS

SMILE FOR THE CAMERA

It was Picture Day at school. Little boys who normally have disheveled hair had it neatly slicked down. Little girls that usually have unruly, fly-away hair had ponytails and braids that took the better part of their early morning at home to bribe and cajole into compliance. They all arrived at school looking wonderfully … uncomfortable.

As each child took his or her turn in front of the camera, a little boy stiffly held a wooden airplane he had never seen before; a little girl fiddled with the folds or puffs on her fancy dress. The photographer called out, "Hold still now and smile! Look like a super-hero! Look like a princess!" Then a very odd transformation took place. What used to be little faces of pure joy and innocent giggles became intense masks of bared teeth, glassy-eyed stares, and the vacant looks of marionettes that had been abandoned by the puppeteer. The kids were implored to relax and be themselves, but they seemed to have no idea who they really were. Their familiar little world was now on display, and this photographer was a huge imposition.

About an hour later, the kids were all playing outside, laughing, screaming, and racing around the mulch-covered playground. Braids and ponytails were swinging out of their ribbons in delightful tangles; curly hair was bursting out of once

restrictive elastic bands; pant legs were getting muddy, and the pink fluffy dresses were no longer pink nor fluffy. But the smiles were bigger and genuine, and the laughs were loud. Even their eyes were laughing!

In front of the camera, these children were imitating what they've seen all of us do when we know people are watching. We try to be better, whatever that is. We fake a smile, we change our appearance, and we hope a new and improved version of ourselves will be remembered for posterity. We want to look like what we wish we looked like.

Those who love us see the real us. God sees and *knows* the real us. He created us, and He said we are *very* good. There are so many of us who are desperate to redecorate who we are just to get the approval of those whom we barely know.

What if we prioritized our lives the way a child does? At the top of the list, we would be feeling the wind blowing through our hair as we swing as high as we can on the swing set, even though it's Picture Day. We would blow bubbles through a straw in our chocolate milk because it's funny, even though it splatters on our white lace dress. We would tear through the yard in our good pants, playing shark attack or taunting each other with cicadas as we get grass stains on our fancy clothes.

The picture our parents kept in their hearts and the memories they loved to recall were not the stiffly posed photos with forced smiles. They were the pictures of our cute faces, chewing gum stuck in our hair, endless giggles when we were supposed to be asleep – that's what made us who we are.

God already knows when we're faking it. He sees us fall and says, "Aww, she's still learning." He watches us stumble and says, "Hey, that was a little bit better this time." He sees our tears and pain and says softly, "Come here, Sweetie, I want to hold you." He never says, "Can't you do something with that hair?"

Of course, we want to take care of ourselves and be the best version, but it has to be the best version of *us*, not someone else. Is it really a tragedy if I don't feel like putting on make-up? What if I just can't do anything with my hair?

It's time for a family photo. Our Father is in the middle with all of us kids gathered 'round – bunny ears behind someone's head, someone else is sticking out their tongue; someone is pulling the pigtails of someone else who is grimacing in anger, and someone is always blinking! We are all vulnerable and being real. We create so much crying, anger, joy, disappointment, elation, success, failure, drama, yet we get so much love from the Father as He's looking at His kids. We're all here. The real gang's all here.

O God, how desperately You love me! Thank You for always being in the center of my day. Thank You for forming and knowing me. Thank You that I don't have to pretend with You; I *can't* pretend with You! Create a clean heart in me that is steadfast!

In Jesus' name. Amen.

FALLING INTO THE FOAM

I saw an adorable video. A little girl was celebrating her seventh birthday at a local gym. She was hanging with both arms from a very high bar that was travelling all the way across the room over a foam pit. The video was in slow motion, so it was fun to see her little face getting a bigger and bigger smile as she anticipated that drop into the huge pile of foam rubber chunks – and drop she did! I could not believe that tiny little thing had the guts to hang by her hands, unassisted and unharnessed all the way across the huge room! Well, maybe I *can* believe it. She knew that no one who loved her would allow her to do it if it was truly unsafe. Falling into the foam pit was the fun finalé she had been waiting for! Apparently, a lot of other children were waiting for the same thrill, because they were excitedly and fearlessly lined up – how fun!

This tells me we're not afraid of flying. We're afraid of falling hard. Imagine how high we could go if we had no reservations or fear of falling and hitting the bottom hard at the end. It's not the lack of ability that holds so many of us back. It's the fear that we don't have a safe place to land. I didn't say soft … falling from some early attempts at our dreams and goals can make us land pretty hard. I said *safe*. If there's something we're passionate about, it's amazing how hard we can fall and still want to

get up and try again and again. Soft landings mean there's less resistance. Soft landings don't increase our strength nor prove the strength of our passion. But safe – safe means we're still able to try again if we choose to and get stronger along the way. It means we're still alive. Soft landings do get boring, so many of us will begin to test ourselves and become motivated to get a little more daring, to raise our dreams a bit higher, to accomplish more than what we thought we could. Our passions raise our bar of what we consider safe. Or maybe God is raising our faith and trust on what is safe. He knows how high He made us to fly, and He gently nudges us closer and closer to realizing our potential.

Let's go back to the little girl in the gym. When she finally let go of the bar, she fell with as much glee and satisfaction as if she had done a double flip and stuck her landing in an Olympic competition! The falling was just one part of the process, a *big* part of the experience, and it definitely contributed to the motivation to do it again. The video only showed one attempt, but I'm positive she did it again and again.

When we have a passion to use a gift that God has blessed us with, He is a part of the motivation to try again. He *is* the safe foam pit that bounces us back up to the surface. We may not always be smiling like the adorable seven-year-old girl as we make yet another attempt, but with every honest effort and knowledge of Who is catching us, we can hear Abba saying, "Okay, let's try it again together!"

—Psalm 37:23-24

Lord, thank You for the motivation to try what scares me, because I can trust You to keep me safe and hold me tight. Please let me always feel You beside me holding me in every attempt and around me holding me up when I stumble.

In Jesus' name. Amen.

BUT I DON'T WANT TO FREEZE!

One of the little boys in my preschool class loved to dance. When there was some transition time between lessons during the day, we put some music on, and the room was filled with little bodies jumping up and down. They looked like popcorn on the stove. One little guy always wanted the same song. He would hear the very first note of the intro, his face would light up with a smile that stretched from ear to ear, and he was instantly thrown into total joy and perpetual movement. He became Snoopy doing the "happy dance."

One day, instead of letting the song play all the way to the end, I stopped the music and called out, "Freeze!" We were working on listening and responsive skills, muscle control, and the ability to anticipate the unexpected. After a couple of times, the kids got the hang of it, and started to freeze in goofy and creative positions … except for this one little boy. He was caught up in his own little world of happy. He maintained the same smile, the same movement, the same curls bopping up and down. The only difference was, he was dancing in silence while everyone else was frozen into position. I called out to freeze again, but he still wouldn't stop. When he finally realized that he didn't have a choice, he started to cry and said through his prolific tears, "But I don't wanna freeze!" He was afraid that if he stopped, the fun

was over for good. He was confusing being still with stopping altogether – no future fun, no further instructions for anything he could possibly enjoy.

How often do we fail to stop and listen to God for further information? Do we presume we know what's ahead for us, and if we stop what we're doing, nothing else will ever be worthwhile?

We don't always know what's best because we don't know our future. But we can choose to listen and await further instruction.

Being still means perking up our ears and waiting for further marching orders for what's next. It doesn't mean we're sitting in limbo. Being still before God and listening means we can have more confidence that our presumptions aren't taking over what God might be telling us. It means being comfortable with being *un*comfortable. Being still is not shutting out the world; it's letting God in and hearing His voice when He's speaking to us.

Sometimes we get so involved dancing to our own music that we forget to listen to God say, "Freeze!" He may put the music back on and say to keep going, or He may put on different music. Either way, we can't forget to be still for a moment and listen.

—Psalm 46:10

Father God, thank You for always being faithful to guide every one of my steps. Help me to remember to listen for Your voice in all that I do – to be still and always stay in step with You.

In Jesus' name. Amen.

THOUGHTS

HEY, YOU PROMISED!

When you were a child, were you ever given a promise from someone, and then your imagination took you way down the road to an imagined, presumed, perfect outcome? At first, you were so excited just thinking about what you knew you'd be getting, you could hardly wait to have it!

Waiting for a promise is torture for children. The have such a limited sense of time and patience – okay, they have no patience. Adults are really no different. Children consider a promise as a sacred oath that must never, ever be broken. Now, as adults, when we ask someone for a favor or commitment, it's often followed with, "Do you promise?" It's easy for us to forget the human element in making promises. The promise-maker is given no wiggle room in case there's a change in plans. What's that expression we have all learned? "A promise is a promise!" We stake our integrity on it. Do we break our own promises? Often. Are we disappointed when someone else breaks a promise to us? Always. Does God ever break a promise? Never. Ever.

God goes so far as to say that anyone who trusts in Him will not be disappointed nor put to shame. (Isaiah 49:23; Romans 10:11; 1 Peter 2:6; Hebrews 6:18) Wow. Four times. God tells us that four times. Maybe even more, in different ways.

Trusting and waiting are always part of the equation. Patience seems to be a requirement for just about anything that's significant, and it is *always* worth the wait. That's because we don't know the future, and as hard as we may try, we can't control it. We sometimes torment ourselves by trying to make things happen on our own; we often allow ourselves to sink into despair, assuming we have been defeated. Or … we can wait for the promise to come at the right time.

I am not a naturally patient person. I have ruined many batches of cookies because I take them out of the oven too soon (I like to say I like them undercooked, but … no). When I was a child, my mother and I planted some marigold seeds in an indoor planter, and I eagerly waited for them to sprout. Well, I did *not* wait. I killed them, because I kept digging them up to see how they were doing. We can't rush through growing flowers, and we can't rush God as we wait to receive His promises.

If our wait turns out to be longer than expected, be assured God has *not* broken his promise. A promise is made on the terms of the promise-maker. If we take it upon ourselves to change the timing, we will be disappointed every time. God's promises are a sure thing because he already knows the gift will arrive at the perfect time, and His track record is perfect. If we're disappointed, then He's not finished yet. If we decide out of impatience to rush the process, then we can't be angry at the results. The cookies will be raw, the marigolds won't grow, and worst of all, we will miss God's best for us. Timing is everything!

"Those who trust in me will never be put to shame."

—Isaiah 49:23b

*"As the Scriptures tell us,
'Anyone who trusts is
Him will never be disgraced.'"*

—Romans 10:11

*"I am placing a cornerstone in Jerusalem,
chosen for great honor, and anyone who trusts
in Him will never be disgraced."*

—1 Peter 2:6

*"So God has given His promise and His oath.
These two things are unchangeable,
because it is impossible for God to lie.
Therefore, we who have fled to Him
for refuge can have great confidence as
we hold to the hope that lies before us."*

—Hebrews 6:18

Dearest Lord, thank You for not only keeping Your promises, but for assuring me of that fact so many times. You already know how easily I can get discouraged. Please ease my doubt, my unbelief, and my impatience by helping me to write these words, Your words, in my heart and to treasure them.

In Jesus' name. Amen.

BABY VIDEOS

Many people post pictures and videos of their children and grandchildren on social media. I especially love looking at the videos of the babies learning new skills or unabashedly launching into a new experience without the slightest hesitation. They're not even aware that they're being watched; they have no sense of intimidation or insecurity. The closest they seem to come to being wary of something new is waiting and simply staring at someone without reservation until they can imitate the behavior. Then they launch without looking back!

I think that's one reason babies learn so fast, besides having that young, flexible brain. The possibility of failure is not something that occurs to them; looking silly is not in the picture. They want to try, and so they do. If they fail at first, everyone says that they're cute. Ultimately, they are successful so they tackle the next hurdle, and life becomes a series of new things they can grab and master.

So, as we grew and developed, how did we learn to be embarrassed to pursue what we love? Who convinced us that struggling to improve should carry humiliation when we fail the first several times? Why do adults feel that trying and trying is sillier and sillier?

Babies and children get smiles, hugs, cheers, and pats on the back with every effort. But once we are adults, for some unknown reason, our efforts to try something new are often not taken seriously. That puts a premature end to many dreams that could have come true. How sad. What a waste of a gift!

Adults should not give much airtime to others who do not respect the desires of their heart. Having dreams is admirable. Having dreams should be encouraged. And … having dreams is contagious!

Although babies get all the attention on social media, we must remember that *everyone* is *someone's* baby. You are someone's baby. You are God's baby. Everyone deserves the smiles, hugs, cheers, and pats on the back with every effort. Everyone needs someone to be proud of them for trying and trying until they succeed. God says, "Let us not lose heart in doing good, for in due time we shall reap if we do not grow weary." – Galatians 6:9

Paul is addressing adults in this scripture, not babies.

God knows we're not finished until we're finished. He continues to cause us to grow, to strengthen, to learn, and to become more like Jesus every day. Abba is smiling at you, hugging you, cheering for you, and patting you on the back with *every* effort.

—2 Corinthians 4:16

Father, thank You for placing in me the desires of my heart. Thank You for encouraging me to pursue every path, not just to fulfill my dreams, but to fulfill Your plans for me. Thank You for being proud of me and for loving me as Your child.

In Jesus' name. Amen.

THOUGHTS

ARE YOU AFRAID OF THE DARK?

When I was a little girl, I was scared to death to go down into the dark basement alone. I guess I could have turned on the light, but I was still far too aware of the scary things that were undoubtedly slithering through the darkness, ready to grab and destroy me. Nothing good could possibly be in the dark, right? It seemed so empty and , . . well, … dark. I decided it was much safer to run away, rather than take the time to turn on the light.

Here's a thought: Do you realize that our very lives begin in the dark? We develop, grow, get stronger, and more vital in the dark until we are ready to be born and begin a life filled with potential and promise. We may need the sun to keep us alive, but it all began in the dark. Every flower, tree, shrub, even the grass, all start out as tiny seeds that germinate in the dark until they are strong enough to burst through the ground and grow towards the sunlight. Every bird grows inside the dark shell, every reptile, every mammal, every fish – EVERY living thing begins in the dark. Did I mention when God created the universe, darkness was over the surface of the deep until God spoke light into being? Yes, God does some of His best work in the dark.

So rather than being afraid to pass through the darkness, why not go into the dark places of your life with the purpose of switching on the light and grow, develop, and create

something new? Perhaps God wants to use *you* as the light bulb in someone else's life. When we switch on the light and walk down those basement steps, we can see that all those dark places that we thought were so scary are actually just empty areas that God wants to fill with creativity and promise. Maybe there is something He wants to do through *you*!

Darkness has no quantity; it's total emptiness. Emptiness can't be measured either; it can only be filled. Once you are there, the emptiness is gone and begins to fill with light – God's light. So, what are you going to do to fill all the dark places that scare you? Is the future one of those dark places for you? Is it launching a new dream, going to college, starting a new phase of life? Is it maybe overcoming a weakness or a disability? Are you going to run away, or do you want to see what God is going to create in the darkness through you?

—Daniel 2:22

Lord, I confess that I sometimes let dark places scare me, whether it's the dark places in my future or the ones in my past. But I know You bring light and redemption into *every* area of my life – past, present, and future. I want to give myself over to Your creativity, and I trust You to bring Your light into whatever You make with me. I want to be used by You.

In Jesus' name. Amen.

THOUGHTS

HOLDING DREAMS IN YOUR FIST

When my children were little, we lived in a heavily wooded area with a very long, gravel driveway. Although my children rode the bus to school, the walk down and back up the driveway made for a fair bit of exercise.

When my son was in kindergarten, we would wait together for the bus in the morning, and I would meet him at the bottom of the driveway in the afternoon. After many weeks of the same routine, I allowed him to run up the driveway by himself while I unobtrusively kept my eyes on him from the back steps.

One day, I heard him excitedly calling me as he raced up the driveway in his sturdy denim overalls. Just as I started to walk down the steps, he tripped on the gravel and fell, skinning his knee and ripping a hole right through his pants. As five-year-old children do, he wailed loudly, and as I tried to conduct triage, I noticed he was tightly clenching his little fist. I asked him if he had hurt his hand as well as he knee, and through his tears and sobs, he opened his fist to reveal a small pile of tiny Styrofoam beads and said, "The beanbag chair at school had a hole in it, and I brought these beads for you cuz I know you like to do crafts!" My son was so intent on holding on to what was important to him that he kept his priorities locked in his hand, despite his pain, fear, anger, and gallons of tears.

How many of us have let go of the dreams God put in our heart when we experienced pain and frustration? How many of us have thought that our dreams were not worth the trouble when met with a stumble, or fall, or opposition, or had no one to pick us up and conduct triage?

No one who has achieved great things or realized a dream has done so without falling many, many times. Everyone carries the potential for achievement, but too often unforeseen mishaps fool us into thinking "it's just not meant to be." Actually, the struggles make the end product, *you,* much stronger. God knows exactly which spiritual muscles need to be strengthened and defined in us. The struggles mean there were a few hills to climb along the way, and you and God together climbed over them to get where you needed to be. The physical and emotional cost made achieving your dream even more valuable.

If the goal is truly a priority for you, if the passion motivates you to get up in the morning and stay focused with a purpose, then your contribution to the world is what God will use to inspire and encourage others. That makes you an ambassador of the Kingdom of God!

On my dresser I have a tiny box with a jeweled lid. When I open the box, I see a little pile of Styrofoam beads that were given to me many years ago. Some dreams take longer to achieve than others, and it's easy to lose momentum, so every now and then, look inside your own little jeweled box, the one you keep in your heart, and be reminded of the dreams and desires God has put in there. Keep them in your fist with your faith. Nurture them, don't neglect them, and allow God to show you how you are one of *His* jewels. He loves you so much, and He considers you very precious.

—Philippians 1:6

Lord, please give me the inspiration and perseverance to hold tightly to what You have put in my heart. Help me to stay focused, to find strength through the struggles and joy in the journey. I know I can do all things in your strength.

In Jesus' name. Amen.

THOUGHTS

DEEPER AND HIGHER

As I drove down the street one day with my small children in the car, I came to a stoplight, and I mindlessly gazed up at the sky. It was a particularly clear, vibrant blue with a few puffy white clouds wafting above and slowly changing shape. As I was watching, we saw an airplane flying relatively low and another one that was so high it wasn't much more than a tiny dot. A high voice from the back seat asked me if the airplanes were going to crash together. I tried to explain how far apart the planes really were, and I said that things look much different from way up there than they look from down on the ground, but they didn't really understand. They couldn't comprehend the actual height and depth of the sky. They wanted to know, "How far apart are the airplanes? Millions of miles? How far away is the top of the sky? Is the higher airplane at the top of the sky?"

We have trouble comprehending the actual height and depth of God. Our perspective is so limited, so we try to define God's power with things we can relate to, such as "God's love is as high as the heavens above the earth." "Our sins are removed as far as the east is from the west." We have absolutely no understanding of how deep and high God is, because there are no words that would help us understand such a concept. My children once asked me if the bottom of the ocean was the lowest place in the world, or if the roots of plants reach all the way down to the lowest place on earth. They needed to have that definition of deepest, or highest, because it helps them to understand and believe what they can't see. The problem is that adults don't want to believe what they can't see, either.

We believe that we love our children deeply, but if they hurt us, we can carry the anger and pain for life, and the relationship can change. When we first get married, we vow to love our spouses deeply for life, but if they betray us, that love has its limits, and the relationship can be forever compromised. If we are hurt by friends, and if they disappoint us, that love wanes. We have a limit. We betray God on a daily basis, but He has no limit; His love for us only increases. God is in love with us despite the fact that we can never be worthy of His love, so He sent His son to die in order for us to be worthy. No matter what our limited perspective of love is, it does not alter the depth of God. He has no top nor bottom. The same way God's universe is constantly expanding, His love, which is what and who He is, is constantly deepening, broadening, and intensifying without end.

Next time you gaze up into the sky, or down at the flowers, or into the ocean, take a child with you and ask how high or deep our world appears to them. See what kind of limits they set. Then talk about God and see what kind of depth you can describe to them and to yourself; I don't think you can. Try to imagine the limitless love and blessings God has in store for His children, whom He truly, deeply loves. That's just as impossible, but it will fill you with unending awe.

"And may you have the power to understand, as all God's people should, how wide, how long, how high, and how deep His love is. May you experience the love of Christ, though it is too great to understand fully. Then you will be made complete with all the fullness of life and power that comes from God."

—Ephesians 3:18-19

O Lord, it is impossible to fully realize that no matter how big and deep I try to imagine You are, You are always more. Please, Father, let me never cease to be in awe of how wonderful, mighty, and loving You are … towards *me*.

In Jesus' name. Amen.

THOUGHTS

PEEK-A BOO! I SEE YOU!

Peek-a-boo is the very first game a baby learns where he feels very briefly alone, but then learns that Mommy or Daddy is not really gone. She learns to trust that someone is always there and watching, even though she can't see anyone. He knows he can giggle with glee, or whimper with doubt, and the one he depends on *is* dependable.

Have you ever had times in your life when you feel as though you've been playing peek-a-boo with God and He's maybe taking a little too long to reappear? Well, maybe he's not the one who has disappeared and hasn't returned yet.

One of God's truths and promises is that He will never leave us nor forsake us. He says this so many times in scripture you know He must mean business! Why do we sometimes feel that He's disappeared?

Often, we base our evidence of God's presence on how well our lives are going. That's human nature. Even Jesus, in His final hours before His death, cried out, "My God! My God! Why have You forsaken Me?" But God was never more present than in His Son's most painful moments.

If God didn't do what we thought He should have, sometimes we decide to walk away, just so we don't get hurt again.

We can't really *walk* away, because He's always here, so we *turn* away.

God promises that we *will* have trials. He also promises that He will make us stronger through those trials, which will produce endurance, which will produce character, which will produce hope. He promises, and we have known all those promises to be true. So why do we question the one promise God says so many times? Are we afraid to trust Him with that one? Is it too good to be true? One of God's truths is that He *is* faithful and steadfast.

Ask God to help you in your unbelief – to help you in your fear of being left alone, to help you feel secure and "seen" every moment of your life.

Father, please meet me where I am. I want to trust in Your presence and in knowing You never leave. Thank You that You always keep Your promises.

In Jesus' name. Amen.

THOUGHTS

PARTING GIFTS

When I was a little girl, I went to a birthday party for a friend who was from another country. A few days before the party, my mother and I went shopping for the perfect birthday gift. I thought hard about what I hoped she would like, and I was so excited to carefully wrap it in her favorite color paper and hand it to her at the party. She was extremely grateful for the gift, and we all had a wonderful time celebrating our friend on her special day.

The surprise came at the end of the party when it was time for us to leave. She gleefully gathered all of us in a circle, her arms loaded with beautifully wrapped gifts all in different colors. She then announced, "In my country, we give each guest at our birthday parties a present before she leaves because we are so thankful that you are in our lives! Each gift is different, because each of you is different, but if you don't like yours, it's okay to trade!" She obviously was focused on showing her appreciation for what and who she had.

Do we purposefully show our gratitude to God, or do we take for granted the things He gives us every day? Are we grateful for our friends, who are also gifts from God? Sometimes we may think that the things we've worked hard for are not really gifts from God but products of our hands. The truth is,

the preparation, the opportunities, the skill, and the achievement are all gifts that God gives us in different stages. Even the air we are breathing right now without thinking about it is His gift to us.

Being grateful not only helps us to realize just how much God has actually given to us, but it also helps us to handle the trials we go through. Gratitude helps us remember that God is in the business of blessing, and that gives us hope in the midst of the heartache.

—James 1:17

Lord, thank You for all You provide for me – not just my needs, but You bless me beyond my expectations. Thank You for what You have done, what You do now, and what You will be doing in the future.

In Jesus' name. Amen.

THOUGHTS

WHERE'S THE CABOOSE?

I was stuck in my car for fifteen minutes at a railroad crossing, waiting for an extremely long freight train to wind its way across the track. My young children were in the car, and at first, they were excited to see a real choo-choo train! However, after the first five minutes passed, the novelty was wearing off, and my five-year-old son kept asking, "Where's the caboose?" He knew that the caboose meant the end of the train. I kept inching my car forward and craning my neck to see if the caboose was at least in the distance. I figured if I could see how far away the end was, I could prepare myself and the kids for however long the wait was going to be. That was so I could teach my kids patience, so I could be pleasant.

But I couldn't see the end! OH NO! I had to just ... sit there! How could I teach patience?! I was left to wonder, stress out, and incessantly check my watch.

"Mommy, where's the caboose?"

"I don't know! You have to be patient!"

"But Mommy, where is it?"

"It's at the end of the train! Be patient!"

"But I don't want to be patient; I want the caboose! Mommy, what's patient? Are you patient?"

"Gulp."

Isn't accepting the uncertainty of the wait the definition of patience? True patience is dependent on strong faith and the belief that God really does know exactly when the wait will be over. He already knows what's on the other side of the wait. However, often we try to force some element of our own control, because it makes us feel better, we think. The reality of our heart is if we can't see the end, then we can't be in control. For some of us, that's a horrifying reality. But God does always know where the end is, and He seldom gives out that information before we need it.

Patience. Not nervous waiting. Patience. There *is* a better plan ahead. Patience. We can let our guard down without heart palpitations. Patience. There truly is Someone who is always in total control, no matter how long the wait.

If we listen carefully, we can discover that there is a purpose for us in the waiting. We are all waiting for something. We're not waiting for the same thing, but God has custom built our waiting rooms for each one of us. We actually have no idea what will be greeting us when we emerge from that room, but it's always something that we needed and had to grow into.

Sometimes we put a time limit on patience – "I'll give it another hour, and then I'm done!" Patience isn't something to be done once. It takes as long as it takes. I have turned my car around more than once at a train crossing to take a faster way, only to encounter the beginning of the same train on another road, and then I had to wait even longer! If I had not been so impatient, I might have seen what God had for me in the wait, or what danger He saved me from that I never knew.

Relax when you don't see the caboose. We do need patience, but we also need time for the bumpy road that might be on the other side of the track. Trying to outrun the train doesn't work either; God is warning us with bells and flashing lights for a reason.

Lord, I know that You not only have plans for my life, but You are in control of the timing. Help me to rest in *Your* timing and to not try to take matters into my own hands. Help me to see You in the waiting as much as the doing.

In Jesus' name. Amen.

THOUGHTS

GOD'S TREASURES

All of us take great pride in the things we create. We tend to be quite possessive, and we don't hesitate to take ownership of what we know to be ours. That's why we have copyright laws, and we take them very seriously.

Children illustrate this as if their lives depend on it. They may take delight in a surprise gift; they may cuddle a favorite doll or teddy bear, which often ends up in a corner or lost under the bed. But if they have drawn a picture or built a Lego spaceship, they feel as though they have personally participated in the six days of Creation. If they lose their doll or can't settle down without their cuddle toy, their tears will flow until they finally fall asleep out of exhaustion. HOWEVER, when that block tower they have painstakingly built is knocked down, even accidentally, by someone's tiny foot, or their beautiful fingerpainting is ruined by a friend's spilled chocolate milk, the devastation is endless and profound! Ownership evokes a powerful, protective connection that is immeasurably deep. They're just being children acting childish, right?

Do you have insurance for valued items in your home in case they become lost or damaged? Of course, you do; we all do, because some things are very important and valuable to us. When we have special gems or sentimental items, we proudly

show them off with delight – perhaps a loved one gave them to us, or perhaps they represent a great honor or award. We keep them safe in a jewelry or treasure box. Small children have their own ways of guarding their creations, but those cardboard or popsicle-stick boxes are no less important to them than the jewels we have inherited from Grandma are to us.

God calls us His precious treasures. Did you realize that? That is a truth and a concept that seems impossible to comprehend. However, if God calls us *His* precious treasures, He is the Creator claiming ownership of what He has made. He takes great pleasure in our uniqueness because He *did* make us Himself. He didn't find us on the beach with a metal detector or inherit us from a relative. He designed us with deliberate purpose and intent, and He is thrilled with each one of us. After all, He created us Himself, and He is ferociously protective of us – and *you*.

*"Because you are precious in My eyes, and honored,
and I love you, I give men in return for you,
peoples in exchange for your life."*

—Isaiah 43:4

*"They will be My people', says the Lord of Heaven's Armies,
"On the day when I act in judgement, they will be
My own special treasure. I will spare them as a father
spares an obedient child."*

—Malachi 3:17

O Lord, I really cannot comprehend Your great love for me. The closest I can come is knowing the love I have for my own children, or family, or friends. But even that does not come close to Your love. Cause me to remember, every day, in my wonderful moments, in my heartache, that Your love for me gets stronger all the time. Please open my heart to expand with love, like Yours.

In Jesus' name. Amen.

THOUGHTS

COULD YOU REPEAT THAT?

When I was a little girl, I took piano lessons. I was very dedicated, and I did endless sets of scales, and I practiced my pieces constantly because I wanted to memorize them and get better. In school, when working on handwriting, we all had to practice each letter over and over and OVER. I had some bad habits (we all did), so we had to practice those letters until we got them right. I don't think I ever have gotten them right, but that's beside the point.

In the Bible, there are many things that God repeats to us more than once, even multiple times. That's because He wants us to remember, and we're supposed to get better at honoring God and loving each other. Some of the things He repeats are warnings so that we don't keep making the same mistakes. We are still working on those things.

While growing up, listening to repetition was a given. Our teachers knew that if lessons and stories were repeated often enough, perhaps in a different way, we would eventually learn and remember. "One and done" was never an option, because it just doesn't work. Learning from our experiences, especially our mistakes, takes time and thought. It also makes us think twice and possibly reassess what we thought we knew.

God's Word is so much more than the printed word on the page. God's Word is truly alive, and He speaks different things at different times to different people with the same Word. Jesus said things over and over, and He repeated things from the Old Testament again and again. When you re-read the same scripture many times, you often will hear God speak differently, even when the words are the same. That's His power, the Holy Spirit bringing His words alive! If God knows it's necessary to repeat His words, then we know it's necessary to listen.

God says He loves us 310 times in 280 verses in the Bible. Do I need to repeat that?

Dearest Lord, please open my ears to hear You. Let Your soft, loving whispers overwhelm any loud sounds of the enemy as well as the false statements I tell myself. I confess I often do not want to sit and listen to You. Sometimes I say I'm too busy. Sometimes I say I'll do it later. Maybe sometimes I already know what You are going to say and I'm afraid to hear it. I repent of that, O Lord. I want to desire to hear You over and over again. Your voice is the sweetest that I will ever hear. I truly love You, Lord.

In Jesus' name. Amen.

THOUGHTS

GETTING OVER THE HURDLE

When you were a child, did you ever imagine yourself achieving your fantasy future? Did you picture yourself as the hero of your dream scenario? Now move ahead a few years .... Have you decided to pursue your passion, the career you always dreamed of since you were a small child and then embarked on the training, the education, and the lifestyle that will set your course in the direction you want to go? If you have, then great! Don't give up; keep going; maintain your focus no matter what, FORWARD MARCH!

Now several years have gone by, and despite some difficult hurdles, you have persevered and seem to be moving along well. You have planned, worked so very hard, and you are now getting excited as you can see your goal coming into view on the horizon. All of a sudden, without any warning at all, crisis rudely bursts on the scene! It's not anything you did wrong; you have gotten some very bad news, or there's been a natural disaster, or an unexpected family issue, or a serious illness. Your dream is stalled, and your heart and soul have taken a beating with an intensity that you have never experienced or even thought about before. Within a few seconds of getting the news, an entire series of presumed scenarios floods your mind, and you feel as though your entire future has been ripped away, like someone has torn

all the pages out of the book of the rest of your life. Okay, deep breaths …

Let's take a look at the reality of life. Considering the fact that we are all imperfect human beings, *all* plans must be made remembering that God knows our future, and He also knows how to prepare us for it. When we first set out on the exciting path we plan, we are like small children – our dreams are big, but our experience is small. We imagine ourselves valiantly trudging up the mountain, amid groaning, sweating, being brave, ready to do what it takes. We really have no idea what it takes. We forget that it might take a few falls backwards. Sometimes those falls can be pretty hard and leave significant cuts and bruises, but our Father is always catching us and helping to stand us up, point us in the right direction, and give us a push. That's because our stumbles are not failures; they are training experiences that God knows we can master. My dad ran beside me when I was learning how to ride a bicycle. I fell a lot, even though he was standing there. He didn't let me crack my head open, but he did know I was going to fall, and I finally mastered the task at hand.

God is standing right there beside us when we stumble. All those speed bumps, hills, and mountains are hiding unknown treasures to discover on the other side, and He is making sure we get there. Just put your helmet and elbow pads on.

Lord, thank You for designing a special plan for me, even before I was born. Help me to make my plans with wisdom; help me to listen to Your voice and hear You guiding me. I want to commit my plans to You, and I want You to guide my footsteps.

In Jesus' name. Amen.

THOUGHTS

DANCING SQUIRRELS

Children make such a dramatic change from their first semester of preschool to the second semester. When visitors come the second half of the year, they often have no idea of the growth and change that has occurred. The little ones arrive early in the morning, excited to see their friends. They joke around, and they proudly show off new shoes or backpacks. In short, they are confident in who they are.

The first week of school is a bit of a different story. They cling to Mom or Dad as if they will never see them again; little faces are contorted in fear; there are so many tears, even a few tantrums. They have entered into "fight or flight" mode, and most would choose flight if they could. They do *not* want to be left alone; they're in a panic, and they don't know which way to turn. They just want to run … somewhere.

Have you ever been driving down a neighborhood road just as a squirrel starts to run across the street? It darts out, sees your car, and then begins the squirrel dance. He zigs to the right! Sharply, he turns to the left! He starts to run back to the curb! Nope, bad choice, so he tries to dart across again! Right! Left! Back! Forth! Zoom! In any direction! Panic! Panic! Panic! Got the picture?

Some children start their growing up journey like dancing squirrels. They're curious, eager, impetuous, and they race forward without looking around. Suddenly, they see something big and scary looming close, and they begin their own squirrel dance, often running back to Mom and giving up out of fear. They allow fear to take away their motivation to dream and explore. God wants us to enjoy all He has created and provided for us. He wants us to trust our connection to Him and run towards our dream instead of doing the panicky squirrel dance and running back to the curb. He knows the joy and confidence we will have if we keep moving forward. Just like second semester kids in preschool, once we have the confidence that our loving Father will always be right beside us, supporting us, we will be happy where we are going and how much we are growing!

Lord, I thank You for putting dreams, desires, and goals in my heart. Help me to serve and honor You with those desires. Help me to conquer fear when those desires require me to confront big obstacles.

In Jesus' name. Amen.

THOUGHTS

IS PERFECTION PERFECT?

I was talking to a friend about her young daughter. This mom was frustrated because her daughter wouldn't try new things because she was afraid of failure. "She's a perfectionist and doesn't want to do anything wrong!"

As a teacher, having a student who is afraid of failure is indeed frustrating. Perfectionist kids won't even try to learn what they want to know, because they want to be perfect at it first. But in order to be perfect (whatever that is), they don't want to start off being imperfect. Therefore, they refuse to learn what they need to learn because they don't already know how to do it perfectly! Confused? So are perfectionists. It doesn't occur to them that if they already knew how to do it, they wouldn't be in the class in the first place.

Being attentive to detail, striving for excellence, and always wanting to improve is so very different from perfectionism. What perfectionists miss is that the journey is half the fun, and it's where God teaches us the joy and vision of where He wants us to go. If there is no struggle, there is no strengthening, nor revelation, no AHA! moment. Kids who have learn to stumble and occasionally fall down along their path of learning not only appreciate it more when they arrive, but they learn empathy for others in the struggle.

God knows we can't be perfect. We won't have any idea of what true perfection is until we're in heaven. Our ability and performance have no bearing on how much God loves us. I remember watching my children learn to walk; every stumble of theirs made me love them more, because I saw how they would get up and keep trying until they grew into being on the track team, or on a gymnastics team, or a dancer. God looks at us and sees us as we will one day be in His plans, not as the stumbly people who keep falling down. He knows how we will end up, and until then, He loves walking right beside us as we learn.

Ever go on a hike with a friend? Try going on a hike with your Best Friend Jesus. Enjoy the scenery, and take in the experience. He's got some wonderful things to show you that you would miss if you skipped the stumbly part of your life. The only perfection we can see now is in recognizing God for all He is: He is the perfect Father, the perfect Comforter, the perfect Healer, and the perfect Friend.

*"God's way is perfect. All the Lord's promises prove true.
He is a shield for all who look to Him for protection."*

—2 Samuel 22:31

*"God's way is perfect. All the Lord's promises prove true.
He is a shield to all who look to Him for protection."*

—Psalm 18:30

Thank You, Lord, for caring so much that You tell me more than once, over and over. I love hearing You tell me how Your promises are always true and how I can trust You to take care of me with Your perfect love.

In Jesus' name. Amen.

THOUGHTS

REACHING UP

Children have to start learning how to balance and develop their strength almost as soon as they're born. Thy first have to hold up their heads, then they roll over, they push up on their elbows, they sit up, they stand, they walk. Then they learn to ride a bike, roller skate, and continue to grow. With every new development, in every area of growth, they must first learn to balance. They try, they fall, they try, they fall again; they keep stumbling until they make it. Something in them motivates them to keep trying. Some intrinsic goal keeps pushing them forward. They don't get embarrassed when they fall; they barely seem to notice that people are watching. They may cry if the fall is hard, but they never stop pushing forward and up – and up.

Why do we lose this motivation to keep moving up to the next level? God puts in us the desire to never stop learning and growing, but we squelch it and tamp it down. We look from side to side to see if anyone saw us stumble, we say we're too tired to try again, or even worse, it's not worth the trouble. And we stop.

God wants to rekindle your love, your motivation, and your pursuit of Him. He doesn't want us to settle, but to continue to push up and out. Don't even look from side to side to see if anyone saw you fumble a bit. Everyone else is too busy fumbling themselves. If anyone else is watching, it's because they're

stagnant and stuck, which is why they have time to judge someone else.

We know God never intends for us to stop growing, because he says that "even unto our old age we will be full of sap and very green." Sap is the blood of a tree, and being very green means we still have much to learn, discover, and will bear so much fruit.

A child is always learning and growing. God calls us His children for a reason; He wants us to be always learning, growing, and reaching up to Him and, like trees, to have our green branches reaching out to others. It is *never* too late, and it is *always* worth it, because it's for Abba, and Abba is always for us.

*"Even in old age they will still produce fruit;
they will remain vital and green."*

—Psalm 92:14

Father, please inspire me, motivate me, excite me to continue reaching up, growing, learning, to use every bit of blessings You have given me. Let me never tire of reaching to You.

In Jesus' name. Amen.

THOUGHTS

MONSTERS IN MY ROOM

My children used to call out to me at night long after I thought they had fallen asleep, "Mommy! I keep thinking about monsters! I'm afraid of monsters! I can't sleep!" So, I would go into their rooms with a bottle of the cheapest, most pungent cologne, also known as monster spray, liberally squirt it throughout the room, and they would blissfully drop off to sleep with that lingering smell keeping them safe for another night. They were focusing on the smell, never being aware that Mommy and Daddy were close by, and God was even closer.

Do you ever have anxious thoughts, or grown-up monsters, that keep you awake at night? When you try to stop thinking about that one thought that is eating you up, you think about it even more. You don't want to be awake all night, but if you could just think through and solve that one problem, or make sure that person who insulted you apologizes, you will be able to relax and fall asleep. Easy.

Not so fast. Focusing on your problem and how you are going to solve it will not help you sleep. Focusing on how you want God to solve your problem won't help either. But what if you focused on God – just God? What if you focused on His truths, His love, and all the ways He has never forsaken you?

It is mentally impossible to focus on more than one thought at a time. We may think we have the dubious gift of thinking many thoughts at once, but we're really just switching thoughts back and forth at lightning speed, hence the insomnia.

I heard about an interesting little trick: Look around your room and find five things that are blue. Look at them, focus on them, memorize them, ingrain them in your memory. Now close your eyes, and keeping them shut, try to remember everything in the room that was green. What? But You were focusing on blue! You weren't noticing the things that were green! However, they were there the whole time!

All the blue things are the things we focus on – the bad thoughts, the lies we tell ourselves, the hurts, the insults. The green things are God and all the things we know about Him. God is here the whole time, but we don't focus on Him; we focus on the scary stuff.

God wants us to focus on Him, remember Him, to know and be aware that He is here the whole time. We can choose to focus on the scary stuff or we can choose to focus on God. Yes, you *can* help it. Yes, you *do* have a choice. You are the boss of your thoughts, which is another gift of God.

God is Light, and as soon as He begins to come into view, the darkness no longer exists. God is the green that has been here the whole time; He's the lingering scent that pushes away our mental monsters. He wants us to retain the childlike part of us that calls out to our Abba in the middle of the night when we are afraid, or when we can't sleep, or when we don't want to be alone. He wants us to run to Him when we are excited, because He's the reason for our joy. And He wants us to come to Him as a child, because we *are* His beloved children.

*"Don't worry about anything; instead, pray about everything.
Tell God what you need and thank Him for all He has done.
Then you will experience God's peace, which exceeds anything
we can understand. His peace will guard your hearts and
minds as you live in Christ Jesus. And now, dear brothers
and sisters, one final thing. Fix your thoughts on what is true,
and honorable, and right, and pure, and lovely, and admirable.
Think about things that are excellent and worthy of praise."*

—Philippians 4:6-8

Dearest Abba, I want to focus on You. I want to dispel the monsters in my mind. I want to put my problems in the proper place in my mind. Cause me to remember that the thoughts and truths about You, and Your power, and Your peace, and Your love, will always overshadow any problem I could possibly have. You know about those problems before they ever happen, and You already have the solution. Please help me to focus on that – on You. None of my monsters have ever been or ever will be any match for You. Thank You for being my Lord, my Father, my Abba forever.

In Jesus' name. Amen.

AUTHOR BIOGRAPHY

Robin Conrad Sturm began her ballet training at the Washington School of the Ballet and is a graduate of the Academy of the Washington School of the Ballet. She was a principal dancer with the Washington Ballet, of which she was a founding member. As a principal dancer with the Washington Ballet, Ms. Sturm originated many lead roles and performed principal roles in the company's repertoire. She also appeared as a soloist dancer in Jerome Hines's opera, "I Am the Way," at the Bolshoi Theatre in Moscow.

Ms. Sturm has been on the ballet faculty at the Washington School of the Ballet and the American University in Washington, D.C. She was a principal dancer and artistic director of the Asaph Dance Ensemble, which she and her late husband, Robert, co-founded, as well as the founder and artistic director of the Northern Virginia Dance Academy. Her experience in the world of ballet as a dancer and teacher and working with children for the majority of her adult life is what inspired her writing of her earlier books. Ms. Sturm is now a certified Children's Life Coach, and she now assists/teaches in a preschool, which has become her latest inspiration in her writing for and about children.

She has three grown children, Jeremy, Rebekah, and Samantha, and lives in Manassas, Virginia.

Ms. Sturm is a recipient of Prince William Living's Most Influential Women Award of 2020. She has also received Insidenova's Best of Prince William Award as Best Author of 2018.